curious about

# WILDFIRES

BY DEBORAH SCIGLIANO

AMICUS LEARNING

# What are you

# curious about?

CHAPTER THREE

## Escaping a Wildfire



Curious About is published by
Amicus Learning, an imprint of Amicus
P.O. Box 227, Mankato, MN 56002
www.amicuspublishing.us



Editor: Ana Brauer
Series Designer: Kathleen Petelinsek
Book Designer and Photo Researcher: Kathleen Petelinsek

Library of Congress Cataloging-in-Publication Data
Names: Scigliano, Deborah A., 1951– author
Title: Curious about wildfires / by Deborah Scigliano.
Description: Mankato, MN : Amicus Learning, an imprint of Amicus, [2026] | Series: Curious about extreme weather | Includes bibliographical references and index. | Audience: Ages 6–9 | Audience: Grades 2–3 | Summary: "Why do wildfires get so big? Learn the causes and effects of one of nature's most powerful and destructive events in this question-and-answer book for elementary-aged readers. Includes infographics, table of contents, glossary, books and websites for further research, and index"— Provided by publisher.
Identifiers: LCCN 2025012835 (print) | LCCN 2025012836 (ebook) | ISBN 9798892008440 library binding | ISBN 9798892009102 paperback | ISBN 9798892009768 ebook
Subjects: LCSH: Wildfires—Juvenile literature
Classification: LCC SD421.23 .S35 2026 (print) | LCC SD421.23 (ebook) | DDC 363.37/9—dc23/eng/20250721
LC record available at https://lccn.loc.gov/2025012835
LC ebook record available at https://lccn.loc.gov/2

Photo Credits: Alamy Stock Photo/Adam DuBrowa/FEMA, 13, Imago, 21; envato/polshindanil, 17, 20, 21, 22, 23; Shutterstock/absolutimages, 18, Alaskagirl8821, 16–17, Bildagentur Zoonar GmbH, 5 (second from bottom), Brian Gailey Photography, cover, 1, David A Litman, 6–7, David Pereiras, 3, 19, Donn Fuller, 2, 9 (bottom), EWY Media, 2, 15, Feng Yu, 18, jannoon028, 5 (top), Natalia Leinonen, 5 (second from top), New Africa, 11, Pixel-Shot, 18, Ringo Chiu, 9 (top), Roman Mikhailiuk, 4, serhii.suravikin, 11, Simun Galic, 10–11, Tatiana Popova, 5 (middle), Toa55, 14, zimmytws, 18, Zyphyrus, 5 (bottom); Wikimedia Commons/Frank Schulenburg, 20, Internet Archive Book Images, 20, Minnesota Historical Society, 20, U.S. Forest Service- Pacific Northwest Region, 20

# CHAPTER ONE

# What causes wildfires?

Lightning strikes are a natural cause of wildfires.

People cause about 90 percent of them. Unattended campfires can spread. **Arson** is when a fire is started on purpose. About 10 percent of wildfires happen because of natural causes, like lightning or lava. Human-caused fires burn more quickly. They spread twice as fast. They kill more trees.

## HUMAN CAUSES OF WILDFIRES

CIGARETTES

CAMPFIRES

ARSON

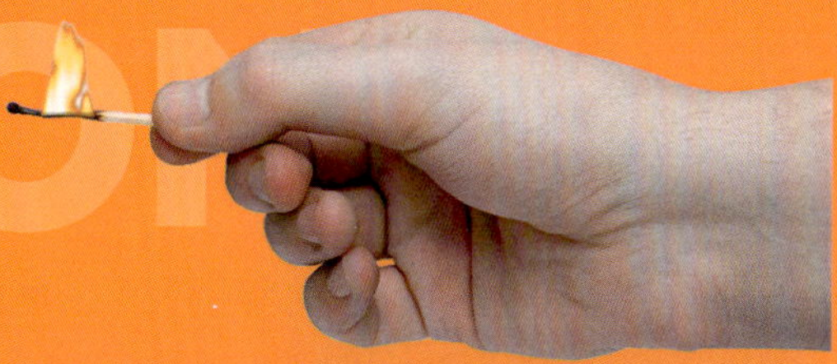

FIREWORKS

DOWNED POWER LINES

# Where do wildfires happen?

Dry, windy areas are at the highest risk for a wildfire.

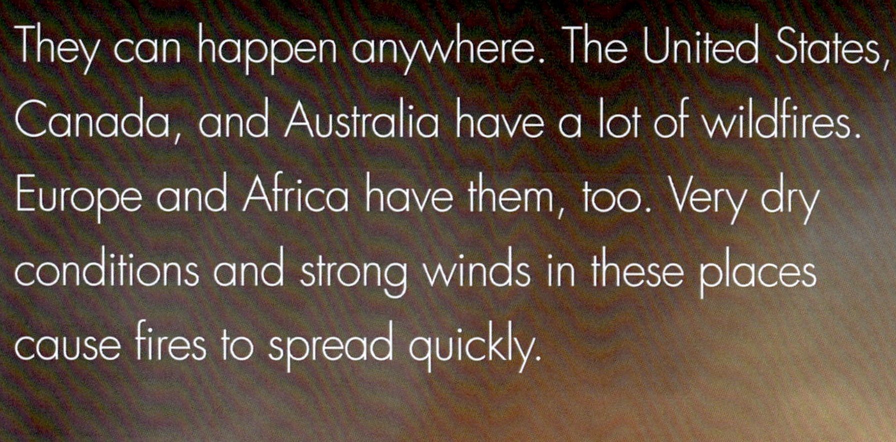

They can happen anywhere. The United States, Canada, and Australia have a lot of wildfires. Europe and Africa have them, too. Very dry conditions and strong winds in these places cause fires to spread quickly.

# What happens in a wildfire?

Wildfires burn trees and homes. They spread quickly and put people's lives in danger. Animals can be harmed. They lose their **habitats**. Wildfires burn millions of acres (hectares) a year. The smoke contains harmful particles. This can cause irritated eyes and breathing problems.

In 2025, the Palisades Fire caused damage in a part of Los Angeles, California.

## DID YOU KNOW?

Sometimes wildfires are good. A controlled burn helps clear the forest floor and kills diseases that harm the wildlife.

A controlled fire clears old plants so new ones can grow.

CHAPTER TWO

2

# How do firefighters help put out a wildfire?

This plane is helping put out a wildfire from above.

Some firefighters parachute into a fire. They are called smokejumpers. They clear the way for ground crews. Firefighters use portable pumps and tank trucks. Planes dump water or chemicals on fires. **Drones** also help in fighting wildfires. They show where the fire is spreading.

## FIREFIGHTING TOOLS

# Can rain help to put out wildfires?

Sometimes. A lot of rain can help. But the fire may be too big for rain to stop. Rain can help clear wildfire smoke from the air. Too much rain on burned land can start **landslides**.

Heavy rain after a wildfire can cause the ground to slide and damage highways.

# Can we stop a wildfire from happening?

Drones help firefighters know where a fire is burning.

Kind of. Clearing **debris** and being careful with flames can help. **AI** drones could help stop wildfires. They are the size of planes. They can carry water. They could spot fires and put them out. AI drones are still being tested by scientists.

## DID YOU KNOW?

**Smokey Bear is a mascot used by the U.S. Forest Service to spread awareness about wildfires.**

CHAPTER THREE

3

# Why do wildfires get so big?

Wildfires can move fast and change direction with the wind.

The fire triangle shows the three things needed to make a fire burn.

A fire needs fuel, heat, and oxygen to burn. Dry grass, trees, and leaves provide fuel. Lightning and campfires are heat sources. Wind carries extra oxygen. Strong winds cause fires to spread quickly. Fires can spread faster than 14 miles (22.5 kilometers) an hour.

# Can you escape a wildfire?

Yes. Local officials may ask people to **evacuate**. People should leave when they are asked. This will help them to escape. Families should have an evacuation plan. Pets need to be part of the plan.

## WILDFIRE "GO KIT"

It's important to have a plan before a wildfire starts.

**MATHESON FIRE**
Ontario, Canada
Year: 1916
223 killed

**CLOQUET FIRE**
Minnesota, US
Year: 1918
More than 1,000 killed

**CAMP FIRE**
California, US
Year: 2018
86 killed

**PESHTIGO FIRE**
Wisconsin, US
Year: 1872
More than 1,500 killed

# What was the worst wildfire?

The largest happened in Russia in 2003. It destroyed more than 55 million acres (22 million hectares). The costliest wildfire was the Camp Fire in California in 2018. It cost $16.5 billion in damages.

## STAY CURIOUS!

# ASK MORE QUESTIONS

**What happens to animals caught in a wildfire?**

**How can we keep our house safe from wildfires?**

**Try a BIG QUESTION: Can homes be built that won't be damaged by fire?**

# SEARCH FOR ANSWERS

**Search the library catalog or the Internet.**
A librarian, teacher, or parent can help you.

**Using Keywords**
Find the looking glass.

**Keywords are the most important words in your question.**

**If you want to know about:**

- helping animals hurt by fire, type WILDFIRE ANIMAL RESCUE
- keeping your home safe, type: WILDFIRE HOME SAFETY

# FIND GOOD SOURCES

**Here are some good, safe sources you can use in your research.**
Your librarian can help you find more.

## Books

**The Glorious Forest that Fire Built**
by Ginny Neil, 2023.

**Wildfires and the Environment**
by Amidon Lusted, 2025.

## Internet Sites

**National Fire Protection Association: Kids**
*https://sparky.org/#/Sparky*
Learn and have fun with fire safety games and activities for all ages.

**Smokey for Kids**
*https://smokeybear.com/en/smokey-for-kids*
Smokey Bear gives ideas for wildfire prevention.

Every effort has been made to ensure that these websites are appropriate for children. However, because of the nature of the Internet, it's impossible to guarantee that these sites will remain active indefinitely or that their contents will not be altered.

# SHARE AND TAKE ACTION

**Have family fire drills.**
Practice what do to in case of a fire.

**Make fire safety posters.**
Give ideas on preventing wildfires.

**Write thank you letters to your neighborhood firefighters.**
Let them know that you appreciate their work.

# GLOSSARY

**AI** Short for artificial intelligence, technology that performs tasks like a human.

**arson** Starting a fire on purpose to hurt property or forests.

**debris** Dried leaves, grass, and other plants.

**drone** A remotely controlled airborne vehicle.

**evacuate** To go from a place of danger to a safer place.

**habitat** The place where a plant or animal grows or lives.

**landslide** A mass of rock, earth, and trees that slides down a mountainside.

**mascot** An animal, person, or thing that is considered to bring good luck.

# INDEX



## About the Author

Deborah Scigliano is an educator and a writer. She has taught elementary students and college students. She loves to write for children. Science, especially weather, is a special interest of hers.